When I Were a Lad... School Days

When I Were a School Lad...

Andrew Davies

PORTICO

First published in the United Kingdom in 2010 by
Portico Books
10 Southcombe Street
London
W14 0RA

An imprint of Anova Books Company Ltd

ISBN 13: 978-1-907554-14-8

A CIP catalogue record for this book is available from
the British Library.

10 9 8 7 6 5 4 3

Produced by Salamander Books

Reproduction by Rival Colour Ltd.
Printed and bound by G.Canale & C S.p.A

This book can be ordered direct from the publisher at
www.anovabooks.com

Contents

It's A Jungle In There...

They say that your school days are the happiest
days of your life...
Nobody had told Mrs Tomkinson.

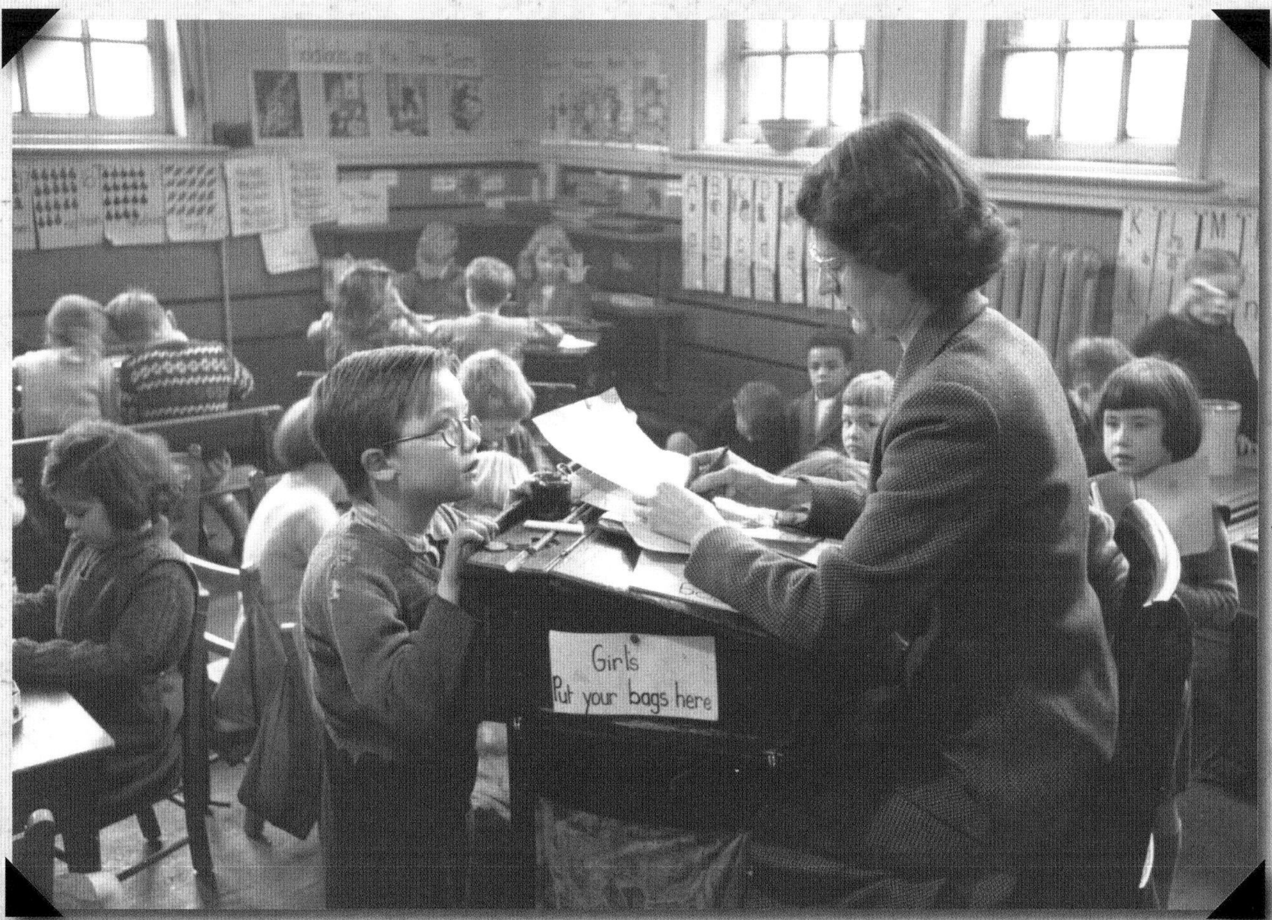
Girls
Put your bags here

We didn't have "phone apps" back then.
We played toss the ha'penny, pitch the farthing
or bowled a hoop. And if you were really
sophisticated and cutting edge -
marbles.

In Autumn we played conkers with no fear
of nasty conker-related injuries or
post-conker conflict anxiety issues.

11

We had free milk, too. But it weren't
ordinary milk.
It were school milk, with school milk taste;
somewhere between yoghurt and
wallpaper paste.

We had respect for our elders. We had respect for teachers and we respected our fellow class-mates who couldn't see as well as us...

Speccy gits!

Kids We Really Hated

Of course there were kids we really hated.
This boy Tarquin insisted on bringing his dog
in and pretending it were his friend Derek.
Derek were rubbish at handwriting.

19

There were Susan Wolstenholme, the most
stuck-up kid in school.
She were full of airs and graces.
Someone told me she never had to empty the
family privvy.
Now that were posh.

21

And then there were kids that looked like
Andrew Lloyd Webber.
That were an easy one.

Or them that couldn't keep their noses out of comics. Who farted constantly.

There were one lad in our school who could fill a gasometer of a morning.

27

School had to take measures in case he let one go near a Bunsen burner.

Then one day a teacher tried to light a fag
in playground and we never saw him again.

31

But the kids we hated most were the ones that enjoyed being stupid. The ones that gloried in being obstinate, rude, unhelpful and thick. They all became coppers.

It Were Always Cold

Kids today don't know they're born. In our day they only turned the central heating on when it got to well below freezing point. In classroom.

35

In them days they thought it was a good idea to spend time outside. If it snowed, even better.

37

You see the trick with snow was always to eat
the white stuff, never the yellow...
But you'd tell toddlers it were lemon flavoured.

Fun With Imaginary Stuff

In them days you had to make your own
entertainment and invent stuff to play with.
Like jumping over imaginary hurdles.

Or leaping over imaginary vaulting horses. Alison Braithwaite broke both knees showing off to camera.

43

In 'Music and Movement' you had to imagine you were a tree, or a stream, or a tiger, or a penguin, or about to be sick.

The girls in the hockey team had an
imaginary overhead wire they all hooked onto.

Then there was imaginary skydiving for
the Air Cadets.

49

Imaginary swimming in our imaginary swimming pool.

51

And you'd imagine if your friends tossed you
in the air from blanket, they might be around
to catch you.
Instead of running off yelling "Surprise!"

Fun With Balls

When I were a lad, you didn't have matching
team kit. No, our first team had shirts from
Arsenal, West Ham, Liverpool, Sunderland,
Millets and the Littlewoods Catalogue.

It didn't help your mental processes heading a leather football with all the bounce of a horsehair sofa.

We reckoned games was a way of getting rid
of kids they didn't want to teach. If you
played footer on a hard surface and made them
strap on squeaky roller skates...

And roller windsailing was a phenomenal success. Provided you had a small hurricane and didn't mind where you ended up.

61

We played cricket, of course, and small Stan had his own set of pads...

...which he wouldn't lend to anyone.
Not even if they were batting.
Bradley Sidebottom never got the hang of
where first slip should stand.

Teachers

Occasionally, you'd get a really soft teacher
and all hell would break loose.

Or you could have some fun with the
student teacher.
"Could you just glue my
rocket please, miss...?"
Some of the teachers were real babes.

69

And some of them looked like men.
If you wanted to find a really vicious teacher
y'had to look no further than a nun.

Lisbon Etados
Lisbôa Unidos
azores D'america
azores

71

Sister Josephine had a cat-o-nine-tails to
enforce discipline.

Sister Theresa swore like a trooper and threw the board rubber, but she were a legend in goal.

Kingdom of the Dinner Lady

When they weren't away with whaling fleet, or
wrestling third bout on the bill at Winter Gardens,
dinner ladies used to dish grub out.

You didn't get a great deal of social chit-chat.
Take your plate and go was order of day.
And you never ever questioned their portions.

Mash were primary ingredient of
every school dinner.
You could never get enough in your
mouth at once.

Once the mash frenzy took hold,
you were gone.

Some lucky so and sos even got battered mash.

And you had to drink every last single precious lingering drop.

Sometimes they let you cook stuff yourself.
That were an adventure.

89

But if the recipe didn't have the word "pie" or "pudding" at the end, you could stuff it.

We had this fat cockney kid at the school who was always goin' on about "larv-lee pasta".

The School Play

Our school plays were so rubbish not even our parents came.

At the time we were surprised. There were some sparkling music on offer.

97

And the costumes had to be seen to be believed.

99

When people saw our version of 'Watership Down'
there wasn't a dry eye in the house.

McVICAR
PHOTO
10-3433-B

101

Of course those b*******s from
'Britain's Got Talent' saw it different.

Rival Schools

If you went to a rival school you
were our sworn enemy.
We hated the kids at Our Lady Immaculate
Fascist School for Girls

And the kids at Scruffside Primary had
trouble written all over them.
Not that they could have spelt anything
with seven letters.

We weren't **that** frightened of them, we just took a few precautions, that's all.

Then there were posh Lady Ursula Hollins school up road. They had lessons in ballgowns. They were so posh they thought "sex education" was all about what you did with sacks.

The boys from Lord Fauntleroy's academy thought
they were so much better than us.
And in many ways they were.
When it came to song and dance
routines we weren't even at races.

Useful Skills We Learned

We learned how to squat in holes.

We learned how to apply
restrictive practices in the workplace
and how to blame our superiors by pretending to
ring them up.

'Start Your Own Siege' were always a very popular after-school class.

The road safety lessons were
frighteningly realistic.

121

Though when a wasp landed on P.C. directing
traffic there was a nasty pile-up
involving three cardboard cutouts and
a tricycle that had to be written off.

We learnt blues harmonica so we could sit on porch, near levee of Humber delta and sing that old "Me Ferret's Got Into Next Door's Laundry Again Blues".

They taught us how to make shapy things
on peggy things...

...How to become an astronaut with two Fray Bentos pie tins and a roll of Bacofoil...

129

...How to become a guerilla artist.
That Banksie started out with the rest of 4H
and Pauline Dodd as his stencil.

You Met All Sorts...

The great thing about school is that you met all sorts. In later life you could avoid them, but for now you were stuck. Like the boy who played invisible keepy uppy for hours.

Giant freaky boy who was 35-foot tall.
He didn't come inside much, but he made a
great centre forward.

Mud boy. He loved mud so much, he rolled in it on way to school.
Every day was like the Glastonbury Festival for him.

Classes were always mixed ability.
While some of us struggled with
true meaning of word "nihilism",
others had fun chalking the letter "B".

139

And we had fat kids, too.
People today think they invented fat kids but
we had fat kids way back.
And we didn't blame society's fast food
culture for their eating challenges either - we
blamed their greedy fat pudgy fingers.

School were an education that's for sure, but they weren't the happiest days of your life. No way. 'Cos you spent twelve years praying very hard that life after school was going to get a whole lot better...

Picture Credit Where Picture Credit's Due

Pictures courtesy of **Getty Images:** Pages 7, 9, 11, 13, 14, 17, 21, 33, 35, 37, 39, 41, 44, 47, 51, 59, 61, 67, 71, 72, 77, 79, 83, 85, 87, 91, 93, 97, 109, 117, 121, 127, 129, 130, 133, 135, 137, 143, 144. **Topfoto:** Pages 27, 31, 57, 63, 64, 69, 75, 81, 105, 107, 111, 114, 123, 141. **PhotoShot:** Pages 19, 29, 43, 89, 103, 113, 139. **Rex Features:** Pages 24, 49, 54, 95, 99, 101. **Corbis:** Pages 23, 53, 113, 124. Picture research: Frank Hopkinson and Rebecca Sodergren (right).

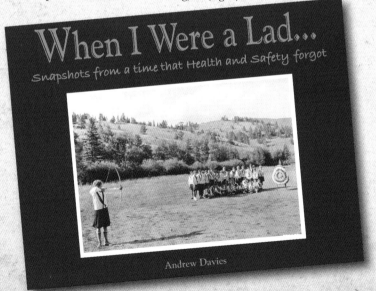

If you liked this, you might like to try; *When Were a Lad …* From a time when kids played conkers, footer boots were made for clogging and you could throw snowballs without filling in a risk assessment report. Take a nostalgic trip back to a time when children got dirty, wandered around on their own and occasionally cuddled vermin.

ISBN 13: 978-1-907554-00-1